STEAM DAYS ON BR

THE MIDLAND LINE IN SHEFFIELD

by

PETER FOX

Published by Platform 5 Publishing Ltd., Lydgate House, Lydgate Lane, Sheffield S10 5FH, England.

Printed by BDC Printing Services Ltd., Slack lane, Derby, DE3 3FL.

ISBN 1 872524 16 8

INTRODUCTION

This book aims to present a record of the train services on the Midland line in Sheffield in the BR steam era. It is not intended to be a comprehensive history of the line. Nor is there room in a small book like this to deal in detail with matters of infrastructure – stations, yards, sidings etc. Thus the book concentrates on the train services operated and their motive power.

It is hoped that a proper history of the railways in Sheffield can be produced at a later date, and anyone interested in contributing to this should contact the author at the address shown on the title page.

HISTORICAL BACKGROUND

The original North Midland route from Derby to Leeds avoided Sheffield, mainly because it was constructed as a coal railway and therefore followed the easy Rother Valley route from Chesterfield to Rotherham. It was opened on 11th May 1840 from Derby to Masborough and was extended to Leeds on 30th June of the same year. The first railway in Sheffield was that of the Sheffield and Rotherham Railway from Sheffield (Wicker) to Rotherham (Westgate) opened on 31st October 1838. A later branch from Holmes Junction to Rotherham (Masborough) (opened 1st May 1869) meant that it was possible to connect at Rotherham with the North Midland Railway's trains.

The Sheffield, Ashton-under-Lyne and Manchester Railway's line from Manchester (London Road) to Sheffield Bridgehouses was Sheffield's first main line, opened in 1845, but it was not until 1st February 1870 that the Midland Railway built its Sheffield deviation. This diverged from the original North Midland route at Tapton Junction (just south of Chesterfield) and joined the Sheffield and Rotherham line at Grimesthorpe Junction.

The Midland Railway opened the Dore and Chinley line on 1st June 1894, thus providing an alternative route to Manchester to that of the Great Central, as it linked up with the Derby–Manchester route at Chinley. Finally, the line from Wincobank Station Junction to Barnsley (Quarry Junction) was opened on 1st July 1897.

A scene at Sheffield Midland station on 18th March 1961. Jubilee Class 4–6–0 No. 45649 'HAWKINS' runs into Platform 1 with the 7.54 am Worcester–York. On Platform 2 can be seen the 11.38 am Sheffield–Leeds local service. One of the two signal boxes on the platforms, 'A' box, can be seen on the right.
Peter Owen Jones

MAPS

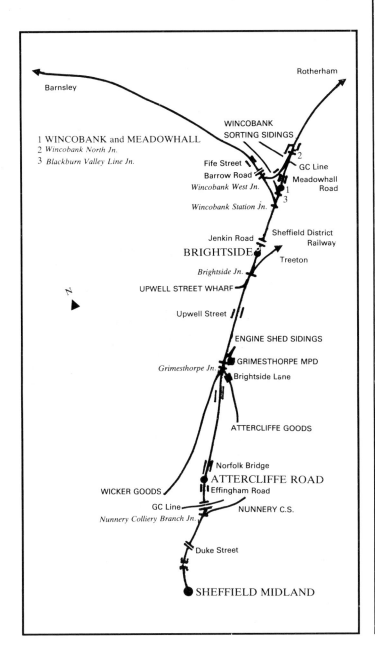

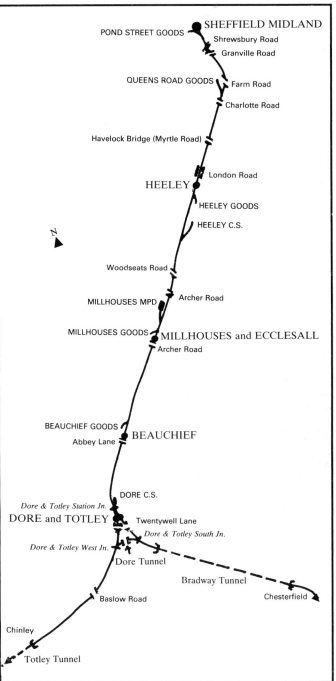

TRAIN SERVICES

EXPRESS PASSENGER

Express services consisted of two basic types – those to London St. Pancras and those on the North East–South West axis.

The London trains generally ran to and from Bradford Forster Square, with some terminating at Sheffield and four trains (two daytime and two nightime) running to and from Scotland, the most famous of these being the 'Thames–Clyde Express' to Glasgow. The other daytime train (to Edinburgh) was known as the 'Thames–Forth Express' before the second world war, but in post-war days ran nameless until 17th June 1957, when it gained the title of 'The Waverley' (after the Waverley route which the train followed from Carlisle to Edinburgh).

The North East–South West services ran from either Bradford, York, Newcastle or Sheffield and mainly terminated at Bristol, but the 'Devonian' ran through from Bradford to Paignton (Kingswear on summer Saturdays) and there was also one return working between Newcastle and Cardiff (the best patronised train on the route). Through carriages to Bournemouth West were carried on a Sheffield to Bristol service and attached at Birmingham (New St.) to the 'Pines Express' which ran via the Somerset and Dorset line. In summer, a separate Sheffield–Bournemouth train replaced these through carriages departing from Sheffield at 10.10 am. In addition, many additional trains ran on summer Saturdays (see pp. 50/51).

One interesting routing was that of the up 'Thames–Clyde Express' which used the deviation between Cudworth and Monk Spring Junction (just south of Barnsley) rather than the more usual route via Rotherham.

LOCAL PASSENGER

Local services ran on the main line to Leeds with the odd train being extended to Bradford Forster Square. To the south, trains ran to Derby and Nottingham, the latter trains continuing along the Erewash Valley Line to Long Eaton (the real Long Eaton, not the current Long Eaton which used to be called Sawley Junction) before turning east to call at Attenborough and Beeston. The expresses, however, used the shorter route through Radford.

Branch trains ran from Sheffield to Barnsley (Court House) and from Sheffield to Chinley via the Hope Valley Line. Certain of the Hope Valley trains ran through to Manchester Central via Romiley and Stockport Tiviot Dale. There was only one express train on this route, at 8.05 am calling only at Hope, Edale, Chinley and Manchester Central.

The line to Rotherham Westgate closed on 6th October 1952, the remaining local trains being diverted to Masborough. Another 1950s service withdrawal was that of the line from Cudworth to Barnsley (closed 7th June 1958). Certain local trains used to run from Sheffield to and from Barnsley via Cudworth, but these were then cut back to Cudworth.

▶Because Heeley station was situated between the carriage sidings and Sheffield Midland, excursion trains tended to start there. The notice shows excursions to Scarborough, Cleethorpes, Skegness and Belle Vue. *Peter Fox*

▶▶The excursion trains were well patronised from Heeley. *Peter Fox*

FREIGHT

Freight services were sparse through Sheffield Midland, the majority of through freights using the original North Midland route (the 'Old Road'). However, sidings and goods yards were to be found all over the place. The main Midland goods depots were at Wicker and Queens Road, with another ex-LMS depot being found at Wharf Street. This was built by the London and North Western Railway and was served by means of running powers from the LNWR-GNR joint line in Leicestershire over the GNR and GCR. It is thus not relevant to this book. The various sidings were served by trip freights, notably 81 trip (operated by Millhouses MPD) and 82 trip (operated by Grimesthorpe MPD).

The majority of freights to be viewed south of Sheffield were bound for the Hope Valley route and generally terminated at Gowhole yard, west of Chinley. Freights to Gowhole also ran from Avenue Sidings, south of Chesterfield via the south curve at Dore.

In the days of steam, most freight trains consisted of 'unfitted' wagons, i.e. wagons not fitted with continuous (vacuum) brakes. The Midland line had, in addition, an overnight network of 'fitted' freights, the northbound workings of which could be seen in daylight hours. The best known of these was the Leicester–Carlisle, which passed through Sheffield Midland at 7.23 pm. This swapped portions at Rotherham Masborough station yard with freights from Somers Town (adjacent to London St. Pancras) and Sheffield Wicker.

PARCELS & OTHER PASSENGER-RATED TRAFFIC

Lastly, no summary of train services would be complete without mentioning the various non-passenger services which were officially passenger-rated and used passenger stations. These included various overnight parcels and mail services between London and Bradford, Newcastle and Bristol etc., the latter two places being served by the travelling post office (TPO). Another important traffic was milk from the Express Diary at Appleby (Westmorland). This was conveyed to London on the Carlisle–Cricklewood milk – a train of six-wheeled milk-tanks, complete with an LMS six-wheeled passenger brake van (generally known as 'Stove R's). Incidentally, one of these six-wheeled milk tanks were often seen stuck on the back of the up 'Waverley'!

Express services were run up the Hope Valley route on summer Saturdays to Bangor, Llandudno and Blackpool. Stanier Class 5MT 4–6–0 45265 of Saltley depot heads a mixed rake of LMS coaches with the 10.40 am Sheffield–Llanudno in 1957.

David Marriott

MOTIVE POWER

MAIN LINE PASSENGER

The staple motive power for express services was the fleet of 'Jubilee' Class 4–6–0s allocated to Leeds Holbeck, Millhouses, Kentish Town, Derby, Nottingham and Bristol Barrow Road. These worked the principal services and were supplemented by Stanier and BR standard Class 5MT 4–6–0s. Holbeck and Bristol had Stanier Class 5MTs with inside Caprotti valve gear allocated and their typical staccato exhaust sound as they slogged their way up the 1 in 100 gradient from Sheffield to the summit at the south end of Bradway Tunnel will never be forgotten. A solitary Derby-allocated unrebuilt 'Patriot' 4–6–0 No. 45509 'THE DERBYSHIRE YEOMANRY' also appeared from time to time. Later on, three such locos were also allocated to Bristol, and regularly appeared on Bristol–York workings.

At times, timing loads for particular trains meant that a pilot engine was required, and this would typically be an MR 2P 4–4–0 or an LMS Compound, but occasionally a Class 5MT was used.

Local services on the main line and Hope Valley line were worked by a large variety of loco types ranging from those designed for the job – MR and LMS 2P 4–4–0s, LMS compounds, Ivatt and BR standard Class 2MT and 4MT 2–6–0s etc. to express passenger and larger mixed traffic locomotives on fill-in turns or when they just happened to be available, and freight locomotives, typically MR or LMS 4F 0–6–0s.

Ex-LNER designs were also in evidence, in particular working in from York on North East–South West services. These were generally Class V2 2–6–2s or NER Class B16/3 4–6–0s. The latter also appeared on local trains together with the ubiquitous B1 4–6–0s. Another working for an ex-LNER design was that of a D49 4–4–0 from Hull Botanic Gardens depot. This worked the 9.15 am Hull–Sheffield Midland and the 3.15 pm return train. Interestingly, this service used the 'Swinton curve' between Mexborough and Swinton Town. This curve, closed in the infamous Beeching era, has recently been reopened by South Yorkshire PTE. On summer Saturdays, the Hull–Sheffield Midland train ran an hour earlier and was extended to Birmingham, the motive power south of Sheffield generally being an LMS compound – 4–4–0 hauled throughout! Incidentally, the only other express service on this line to be regularly hauled by a compound in this era was the charter train, the 'C.T.A.C. Scottish Tours Express' from Leicester to Craigendoran which was compound-hauled between Leicester and Leeds.

FREIGHT

Freight trains were hauled by MR or LMS Class 3F or 4F 0–6–0s, or by Stanier Class 8F 2–8–0s, with trip workings in the hands of MR Class 2F or 3F 0–6–0s and later Ivatt or BR standard Class 2MT 2–6–0s. BR standard Class 9F 2–10–0s also appeared, with the very occasional working in mid-afternoon of a Carnforth-based LNWR 'Super D' 0–8–0 on a Hope Valley line freight. Fowler 'Beyer-Garratts' also worked Avenue–Gowhole freights around Dore South

Curve, but the author only ever saw one in Sheffield itself, and then only a light engine.

The Leicester–Carlisle 'fitted' freight was very interesting to local enthusiasts. Diagrammed for a Leicester Stanier Class 5 or BR standard Class 5, this train often had spells of haulage by power from Carlisle Kingmoor (rare in Sheffield), and this would be either a Class 5 4–6–0 or a 'Jubilee'. Consequently this train was probably the most-watched train on the line for those in the know! The later Water Orton–Leeds semi-fitted was almost always a 'Crab' 2–6–0. In the late 50s the workings of the 'fitteds' were changed, so that the Leicester–Carlisle did not run via Sheffield. Its place was taken by a new train, the 4.47 pm. Water Orton–Glasgow, the usual power for which was one of Saltley's three mechanical-stoker fitted 9F 2–10–0s.

THE BARNSLEY BRANCH

The branch trains to Barnsley were worked in the early 50s by Ivatt Class 2MT 2–6–2Ts from Royston depot, 41273/4, which had taken over from MR Class '1P' 0–4–4Ts, but in a surprising move, these were partially replaced in September/October 1954 by two L & YR Class 5 2–4–2Ts (LMS designation 2P) Nos. 50646/50. These left in February 1956, and the service was then worked by LMS/BR Class 2MT 2–6–2Ts 41274/81/2 and 84009 until dieselisation in June 1959. Push and pull working was generally employed and this included an associated working at 7.42 am from Sheffield to Hope, returning at 9.00 am.

SHUNTING & CARRIAGE TRIPS

Shunting at Sheffield Midland was undertaken in early BR days by MR '1P' 0–4–4Ts, the last three being 58079, 58086 and 1370. The latter is interesting because although it was allocated BR number 58086, it still retained its LMS number at condemnation in 1953 although the Ian Allan 'abc' at the time did not acknowledge this! Their duties were taken over by Ivatt Class 2MT 2–6–2Ts 41209/45/46. The 'carriage trip engine' spent most of its life shuttling between the Midland station and the two main carriage sidings at Nunnery and Heeley, plus the two overflow sidings at Dore and Unstone (Derbyshire). Midland Class 3F 0–6–0 43341 had this duty in the early 50s but was replaced by 'Flying pig' Ivatt Class 4MT 2–6–0 43032 in September 1952.

Freight yards were shunted either by MR Class 1F 0–6–0Ts or MR/LMS Class 3F 'Jinty' 0–6–0Ts. One of the former, 41768 seemed to be almost permanently stationed at Queens Road Goods depot until its withdrawal.

LATER DEVELOPMENTS

The delivery of the English Electric Type 4 diesels in 1958 (later known as Class 40s) to the West Coast Main Line resulted in the transfer of Class 7 motive power to the Midland Main line south of Leeds in the form of rebuilt 'Royal Scot' 4–6–0s. Although Leeds

Holbeck had previously had an allocation of six of these, they were normally used on the Leeds–Glasgow section only. The author only remembers two workings of the Holbeck 'Scots' south of Sheffield previous to the 1959 transfer. 46103 'ROYAL SCOTS FUSILIER' was once observed on the down 'Thames–Clyde Express' and 46113 'CAMERONIAN' was once observed on the up 'Waverley' towing a track recording coach on the rear. In the latter case, the extra power was presumably required to maintain a high average speed for testing purposes.

The first two 'Scots' to be transferred were in fact from Holbeck to Kentish Town these having been replaced by two Britannias 70053 and 70054. They were 46103 (above) and 46133 'THE GREEN HOWARDS'. More followed, with Millhouses receiving five plus two rebuilt Patriots. These were:

45514 'HOLYHEAD'
45536 'PRIVATE W. WOOD V.C.'
46131 'THE ROYAL WARWICKSHIRE REGIMENT'
46147 'THE NORTHAMPTONSHIRE REGIMENT'
46148 'THE MANCHESTER REGIMENT'
46151 'THE ROYAL HORSE GUARDSMAN'
46164 'THE ARTISTS' RIFLEMAN'

By the end of 1960, most St. Pancras line expresses were Class 7-hauled, either by 'Scots' or 'Rebuilt Patriots' or by the six 'Britannias' which by then had been allocated to Trafford Park depot (Manchester) for working the St. Pancras–Manchester service. This had become the main route between London and Manchester while electrification work was being undertaken on the West Coast route.

As the Midland lines received more 'Scots', they also began to work services on the North East–South West route, but their reign was short-lived, as from 1961 their services began to be taken over by the BR/Sulzer type 4 'Peak' diesels (later Class 45). They were then relegated to local services and were eventually outlasted by the 'Jubilees'. The Millhouses 'Scots' stayed until the closure of the depot in January 1962 except for 45514 which was withdrawn in May 1961.

Another development was the transfer of LNER designs to Millhouses in the form of Class 'B1' 4–6–0s and later 'K3' 2–6–0s. These were not liked by the Midland crews and the B1s spent most of their time on local services or excursion duties, although they were also used on summer reliefs. On one occasion, even a K3 was used on a Sheffield–Weston-super-Mare working!

The last steam workings on the Midland line in Sheffield were mainly on the Hope Valley line which saw the occasional B1 or Class 5MT-hauled train up to the mid-60s. Express steam had virtually finished by the end of 1962 except for a couple of workings from Bristol and Gloucester to Sheffield, but the bad winter of 1962/3 saw many steam locomotives taken temporarily out of store to cover for failed 'Peak' diesels (or for diesels on which the train-heating boiler was inoperative). By 1964, the only express steam workings were on summer Saturdays (Bradford–Poole north of Sheffield and Manchester–Yarmouth west of Sheffield), but in 1965 the swansong occurred with two Poole trains each summer Friday night/Saturday morning being steam-hauled as far as Nottingham.

►LMS Class 1P 0–4–4T 1370 at Millhouses depot. This loco, which retained its LMS number to the end, was condemned in February 1953.
Peter Hughes

SHEFFIELD MIDLAND TO DORE & TOTLEY

SHEFFIELD MIDLAND. This has always been Sheffield's major station and although referred to as 'Pond St.' on certain Midland Railway maps, it has to my knowledge never actually been known locally by that name, nor referred to as such in timetables, and the constant reference to this in such books as Batty's 'Rail Centres Sheffield' is erroneous.

▲At Sheffield North Junction, Royal Scot 4–6–0 46131 'THE ROYAL WARWICKSHIRE REGIMENT' waits in Platform 1 on 18th March 1961 with the 8.10 am St. Pancras–Nottingham extended to Sheffield, whilst the 'North end shunt' loco, Ivatt Class 2MT 2–6–2T 41245 stands in Platform 2. *Peter Owen Jones*

▶The station shunter in this earlier photograph taken in the early 50s is Johnson Class 1P 0–4–4T 58068. The early 50s Sheffield scene is amply portrayed here, with an abundance of smoky factory chimneys. Rodgers Cutlery works is now part of the new bus station and the building to the front of the loco, Pond's Forge, is now the new Olympic-standard swimming pool being built for the world student games in 1991. *Peter Hughes*

►Ivatt Class 4MT 2–6–0 43032 replaced 43341 as Millhouses's Carriage trip engine in September 1952. In this photograph the loco is seen in original condition in BR lined black livery with double chimney. The double chimneys on these locos proved to be disastrous as far as draughting was concerned and they were all replaced by single chimneys in 1955 (see page 11). The loco standing in the up station sidings between Platforms 5 and 6 at Sheffield Midland.

Peter Hughes

▲In this view taken in August 1954, MR Class 2P 4–4–0 40538 stands in Platform 6 with the 2.45 pm local service to Derby. Behind the engine is an SR CCT and LMS Period 2 (square window) corridor third. LMS compound 4–4–0 41123 of Trafford Park depot stands on Platform 7 with the 2.22 pm to Chinley. Features of interest in this photograph are the original roof which spanned Platforms 5 and 6, removed in the mid 50s and the northerly of the two footbridges connecting Granville Street with the station front. Only the southerly one now remains.

Peter Hughes

▶The carriage trip engine 43032 again, but as rebuilt in 1955 with single chimney. The empty coaching stock train to Heeley Carriage Sidings has just left Platform 5 and is emerging from Shrewsbury Road Tunnel onto the up slow line. The front coach is an LMS Period 1 (twin window) corridor third. *Peter Hughes*

▼The 9.12 am Hull–Sheffield Midland arrives in Platform 5 during 1959 with LNER D49 'Hunt' Class 4-4-0 62767 'THE GROVE' in charge. This was one of the locos fitted with Lentz rotary poppet valve gear. The overall roof in the photograph opposite has been replaced with platform canopies. *Peter Owen Jones*

►The arrival of diesel power in the form of the BR/Sulzer type 4 diesels (later Class 45) rendered the Royal Scots spare and they were often to be found on more mundane duties. Here 46122 'ROYAL ULSTER RIFLEMEN' approaches Heeley on 20th May 1961 with the 9.43 pm Chinley–Sheffield. Heeley Carriage Sidings are just visible in the background to the left of the train. *Peter Fox*

◄Jubilee Class 4–6–0 45668 'MADDEN' storms through Heeley on the same day as above with the 8.50 am Bradford Forster Square–London St. Pancras. This train conveyed through coaches from Halifax via Barnsley. *Peter Fox*

►MR Class 3F 0–6–0 3731 is seen on a trip freight passing under the northerly Archer Road bridge on 12th August 1952. The loco had not then received its BR livery and number. *Peter Hughes*

◄A fine view of LMS compound 4–4–0 41114 passing under Woodseats Road bridge with the 5.30 pm Sheffield–Manchester on 30th May 1957. The area in the background is known as Norton Hammer, after an early water-powered tilt hammer which used to be situated in the vicinity. *David Marriott*

▼The Earles Cement works at Hope often used to hire a BR loco when its own loco was unavailable, and this would usually be a MR Class 1F 0–6–0T. This photograph shows 41835 on 24th September 1960, at the time the only remaining 1F to retain a round-top boiler, returning to Grimesthorpe depot after a weeks loan to Earles. It is seen passing under the northern Archer Road bridge. The footpath on the left is the access to Millhouses MPD. Note: although the shedplate is 41D (Canklow), the loco was on loan to Grimesthorpe at the time. *Peter Fox*

LMS Class 5MT 4–6–0 45269 passes Millhouses MPD on 31st May 1955 with the 2.28 pm local train from Chinley. In the background (left to right) can be seen a line up of locos and wagons, the coaling stage, the shed offices and the water tank. The factory of Jacobs (formerly Guylee's) is visible to the right. This firm occupied Millhouses shed after closure.   *David Marriott*

Virtually all standard classes were used on services through Sheffield, the only ones not to appear being the Class 3MT 2–6–0s and 2–6–2Ts, the Class 4MT 2–6–4Ts and 71000 'DUKE OF GLOUCESTER' (and even the latter has recently appeared after preservation!). The only regular working for a standard Class 4MT 4–6–0 was a morning Nottingham–Leeds returning in the afternoon. In 1961, however, the Nottingham services were dieselised and this photograph is of 75063 on 13th May arriving at Millhouses on the 5.25 pm Sheffield–Derby. A pair of enginemen are waiting for a down service to Sheffield.

Peter Fox

The MR Class 2P 4–4–0s were the mainstay of the Sheffield–Nottingham 'Erewash Valley line' local service until dieselisation in 1960. 40337 of Hasland depot is seen between Millhouses and Beauchief on the 5.50 pm Sheffield–Nottingham on 27th May 1957. An early LMS suburban brake third complements the rake of Stanier coaches.

David Marriott

▲An interesting Saturday-only working was the 12.08 pm Cudworth–Chesterfield, which returned e.c.s. to Sheffield. The e.c.s. is seen approaching Millhouses on 13th May 1961 with Royston-based Stanier Class 3MT 2–6–2T 40181 pulling a mixed bag of coaches consisting of a BR standard BS, an LNER Thompson CL and an LMS BS. *Peter Fox*

▶The only push and pull working south of Sheffield was that of the 7.42 am Sheffield–Hope service which connected at Hope into the 8.05 am Sheffield–Manchester express. The loco and stock were a fill-in turn for a Barnsley–Sheffield set. The return working, the 9.00 am Hope–Sheffield is seen approaching Millhouses on 12th April 1957 hauled by Royston-based Ivatt Class 2MT 2–6–2T 41281. The working was discontinued as from 17th November 1958. *Peter Owen Jones*

▲Class 8F 2–8–0 48314 on the Manchester line passes Dore & Totley South Junction in 1953. In the background can be seen Dore Carriage Sidings, used for storage of coaches for seasonal use. *Peter Hughes*

◀Class 4F 0–6–0 43844 at Dore with another Hope Valley line freight on 24th May 1952. Dore & Totley South Junction box can be seen in the background.
Peter Hughes

▶Jubilee Class 4–6–0 45597 'BARBADOS' storms through Dore & Totley with the westbound 'DEVONIAN' on 11th June 1957. On the left just above the end of Platform 1 can be seen the W H Smith bookstall. After the closure of this, newspapers were sold from the waiting room.
Peter Owen Jones

►LMS Class 5MT 4–6–0 44849 with the 8.40 am Bournemouth–Bradford in June 1953. The stock is Southern with the first two coaches being of Maunsell and Bulleid design respectively. Dore & Totley South Junction signal box can be seen in the background.

Peter Hughes

▲Just after nationalisation in 1948, LMS Class 2P 4–4–0 40503 pilots Jubilee Class 4–6–0 45607 'FIJI' on an up express round the curve just south of Dore & Totley station. The tenders still carry 'LMS' livery and the numbers on the 2P are of LMS-style. Coaches are all in LMS livery.

Peter Hughes

►Jubilee 45610 'GOLD COAST' passes Dore & Totley South Junction with an up express on 5th August 1952. This loco was later renamed 'GHANA' when the country gained its independence.

Peter Hughes

▲The spur from Dore & Totley South Junction to Dore & Totley West Junction (known as the 'cutting' to most Sheffield enthusiasts) was used only by freight and excursion trains. Motive power for the freights was the usual Midland line mixture of 3Fs, 4Fs and 8Fs, but the odd Beyer–Garratt also tended to appear until withdrawal in 1958. In addition Class 9F 2–10–0s and Class WD 2–8–0s also appeared. In this photograph, MR Class 3F 0–6–0 43335 emerges from the 88-yard long Dore Tunnel with a mineral train.   *Peter Hughes*

ERRATA: The photograph on page 28 was taken by Peter Hughes, not Eric Slater. In addition, the train has now been identified as the 11.22 am relief from Sheffield to Cardiff on 23rd July 1960.

The photograph on page 29 is, of course, the northbound 'Devonian' not the southbound one as stated.

SHEFFIELD – DORE & TOTLEY IN COLOUR

SHEFFIELD MIDLAND. This view of the South end of Sheffield Midland station c.1956 is typical of the mid 50s. The south end shunt (the Midland station shunters were never called pilots) was Ivatt Class 2MT 2–6–2T 41209, the other two such locos allocated to Millhouses shed for the two shunting duties being 41245/6.

The two Stanier coaches behind the loco are in a bay between Platforms 2 and 5 known as the 'new dock'. This bay was usually used to hold spare stock for strengthening purposes and was not signalled for passenger train working although it is now so used and named 'Platform 2C'. An unidentified Stanier Class 5 4–6–0 stands at the head of a local train in Platform 7. The stone-built slum dwellings behind the station were demolished in the late 50s to make way for the much-criticised Park Hill flats. *Eric Slater*

EXPRESS PASSENGER

▲The main express passenger trains on the Midland line through Sheffield were worked by 'Jubilee' Class 4–6–0s throughout the 50s. 45616 'MALTA G.C.' is seen between Millhouses and Beauchief with the 1.49 pm Sheffield–London on 7th June 1959. This loco was one of the Jubilees fitted with a Fowler tender.

David Marriott

▶The northbound 'Devonian', the 8.45 am Kingswear–Bradford on a Saturday in July 1960 headed by 45685 'BARFLEUR' (with the more usual Stanier high-sided tender) rounding the curve between Dore & Totley South Junction and Dore & Totley station. The policy of allowing greater regional freedom which was instituted by the British Transport Commission at this time resulted in the Western Region deciding to paint the coaches on its named trains chocolate and cream. The train is seen in the transition period with the first coach BR maroon, the second one chocolate and cream and the third one the original BR carmine and cream (or blood and custard as it became known).

Peter Hughes

Express passenger trains for which 'Jubilees' were not available were generally hauled by Stanier Class 5MT 4–6–0s or BR Standard Class 5MT 4–6–0s. This generally applied to summer Saturday additional workings such as the one illustrated above. The locomotive, 44754, is one of the unusual batch fitted with inside Caprotti valve gear. The Bristol-allocated Caprottis were regular performers between Bristol and York or Leeds. They were free-running locos, but found the 1 in 100 climb from Sheffield to the summit at the south end of Bradway Tunnel difficult, especially with the heavy loads that were often the norm with these trains.

The train is a relief from Newcastle to Birmingham on a Saturday in 1960, complete with a rake of LNER coaches of Gresley design (except for the third, fourth and tenth which are of Thompson design), and is seen approaching Beauchief. Beauchief station signal box was generally switched out of use and therefore all signals are in the 'off' position.

Eric Slater

With particularly heavy loads, pilot locomotives were needed, as can be seen with this further view of the southbound 'Devonian' approaching Dore & Totley in July 1959 with Class 5MT 4–6–0 44912 piloting 'Jubilee' Class 4–6–0 45690 'LEANDER'.　　*Eric Slater*

The need for double-heading of heavy trains was alleviated with the transfer of a number of rebuilt 'Royal Scots' to the line. 46157 'ROYAL ARTILLERYMAN' was initially sent to Millhouses, but it had been transferred to Saltley by the time this photograph had been taken. 46157 makes a fine sight on the 12.37 pm Newcastle–Bristol, seen passing Heeley goods on 4th July 1961. *David Marriott*

A number of rebuilt 'Patriot' 4–6–0s were also transferred to the Midland Line. 45540 'SIR ROBERT TURNBULL' allocated to 21A Saltley is seen on the 8.00 am Newcastle–Cardiff passing the steep hillside of Norton Hammer just south of Heeley Carriage Sidings on 28th July 1961. The rebuilt Patriots could be distinguished from the rebuilt Royal Scots at a distance by their side-window cabs and lack of sand-box immediately in front of the cab. There were many other detail differences.

David Marriott

The late 50s also brought Pacifics to the line for the first time in the shape of the 'Britannias'. The up 'Thames–Clyde Express' was not usually worked by one of this class, unlike the up 'Waverley' which was diagrammed for a Trafford Park-allocated Britannia. 70053 'MORAY FIRTH', a Holbeck (55A) loco, is seen on the 'Thames–Clyde' south of Dore & Totley on 9th July 1960. The additional coach at the front of the train is unusual in that it is one of a small number of all-steel Gresley open seconds built by Metro-Cammell in 1927–8.

David Marriott

After the dieselisation of the express services through Sheffield and the closure of Millhouses depot there were no facilities for dealing with steam locomotives at Sheffield. Thus when trains from the North-East arrived steam-hauled because of poor diesel loco availability, the ex-LNER designs carried on south of Sheffield, generally to Derby. One such substitution occurred on 15th May 1964. Class V2 2–6–2 60982 is seen passing Queens Road with the 12.15 pm Newcastle–Bristol. The sixth coach is one of the three Mark 1 griddle cars which were built in 1960.

Peter Fox

The very last express train diagrammed for steam was the 09.06 am Bradford–Poole on summer Saturdays in 1966. This train had been steam-worked only as far as Sheffield during 1965, but the closure of the direct Nottingham–Melton Mowbray route meant that reversal was required at Nottingham Midland, and therefore the Jubilee was diagrammed from Bradford to Nottingham and back. On 30th July, 45562 'ALBERTA' (with painted name) is seen passing the former Millhouses MPD yard. There are no prizes for guessing the identity of the gentleman peering out of the back window of the first coach. *Peter Hughes*

The very last LMS 3-cylinder compound Class 4P 4–4–0 in service was Millhouses's 40907. Two other compounds at Monument Lane had official condemnation dates later than '907', but they had been stored unserviceable for a considerable time. Here we see the celebrated loco south of Dore & Totley at the head of a rake of three Stanier coaches on the 8.12 am Sheffield–Derby local service on 3rd October 1959. *David Marriott*

Stanier Class 5 4–6–0s were frequent performers on main-line stopping services in the area. 45150 is seen just south of Sheffield Midland in March 1966 with the 5.30 pm Sheffield–Manchester Central. The train is formed of a four-coach rake of LMS Stanier stock with an LNER Thompson-designed coach at the rear. To the left of the photograph is the dive-under which brought the down fast line under the two slow lines. It's official name was the 'burrowing junction', but was generally known locally as the 'sough'. To the right are the Farm Buildings, formerly owned by the Duke of Norfolk, but used as the LMS and then BR Sheffield divisional office until the new Sheaf House was built in the mid 60s.

Barry Collins

Another train on the Hope Valley route steam-hauled in the 60s was the 9.39 am Sheffield–Chinley seen here in May 1966 in the same position as the previous photo but taken from the eastern side of the line instead of the west. On the horizon can be seen (left to right) Sheffield Town Hall, St. Mary's Church, the Central Library (the white building) and the two new concrete monstrosities, Sheffield College of Technology (above the cab) and BR's Sheaf House (above the Thompson coach). Note that the position of the top headlamp bracket on this loco and the one opposite had been moved from its previous position at the top of the smokebox to a position lower down on the right to avoid the possibility of accidents when operating on electrified lines. The locomotive is 45059. Note the ganger standing in the 'six-foot'. Yellow high-visibility vests had not been invented then.

Peter Hughes

On 1st August 1959, BR Standard Class 5MT 4–6–0 73074 is seen leaving Dore & Totley on the 4.06 pm Sheffield–Derby. This train was diagrammed for the locomotive off the morning Cardiff–Newcastle train, and was therefore almost always a main-line engine. The second coach is of LMS period II design.

Peter Hughes

LMS Class 4F 0–6–0s were often used on stopping services. 44236 is seen on the 4.30 pm Sheffield–Chinley having just left Heeley on 12th July 1961.

David Marriott

The BR Standard Class 9F 2–10–0s were designed for heavy freight haulage but were often commandeered to work express services on summer Saturdays. 92128 is seen on the 4.08 pm Sheffield–Derby, date unknown, passing the amenities block of Heeley Carriage Sidings. The locomotive will have previously worked to Sheffield on a down express from the West of England. Note the unusual signal between the down fast and up slow lines.

Barry Collins

In 1963 the 9.39 am to Chinley was diagrammed for a Buxton-allocated locomotive. Two types were used, the first type being the Fowler Class 4MT 2–6–4T, a type which had rarely been seen in the Sheffield area in the years prior to this, although there had been a diagram on Sundays in the 50s. 42379 is seen between Woodseats Road and Archer Road on 3rd April 1963. Note the old band 1 'H'-type TV aerials on some of the houses in the background.

Peter Hughes

The other class of locomotive used on the 9.39 am to Chinley was the Ivatt Class 2MT 2–6–0. 46484 is seen approaching Dore & Totley station in late 1963.

Peter Hughes

The Eastern Region's influence was felt by the allocation of LNER-design Class B1 4–6–0s to Millhouses MPD. These were transferred to Darnall when Millhouses closed and later transferred to Canklow. They were mainly used on stopping services, but also saw express train use, mainly on summer Saturday extras and excursions. 61094 is seen on the 12.35 pm Sheffield–Chinley on 9th August 1963 passing Heeley Goods Depot. Note the BR suburban coach next to the engine. The wagons in the siding are conveying timber, probably for Messrs. Arnold Laver & Co., the firm that now has a DIY store on the site!

David Marriott

FREIGHT

In the latter days of the Midland Class 3F 0–6–0s, 43203 is seen with a freight for Peak Forest. The location is the same as on page 36. The wagons present are interesting, with lime wagons much in evidence.

Barry Collins

More powerful were the Midland or LMS Class 4F 0–6–0s, but these locos still found the gradient out of Sheffield a struggle. 44087, an LMS 4F is seen on an Engine Shed Sidings (Grimesthorpe)–Gowhole mixed freight having just passed through Heeley station on 21st July 1960.

David Marriott

The Stanier Class 8F 2–8–0s (and of course the Standard Class 9F 2–10–0s) were the only freight locos that were really man enough for the job of heavy freight on the gradient out of Sheffield. Another Engine Shed Sidings–Gowhole freight is seen at Beauchief station in July 1960 headed by 8F 48178. Beauchief signal box is seen in the background, switched out as usual.

Peter Hughes

The Hughes Class 5MT 2–6–0s were always known as 'Crabs' because of their ungainly appearance. They were to be seen on passenger, freight and parcels workings in the area. 42797 of Grimesthorpe MPD (41B) is seen at the same location as the photograph on page 45 on a mixed freight on 15th August 1960.

David Marriott

ON SHED

Ready for action on Millhouses MPD on 29th November 1961 are Stanier Class 5MT 4–6–0 44775, 'Royal Scot' Class 7P 4–6–0 46164 'THE ARTISTS' RIFLEMAN' and Ivatt Class 2MT 2–6–2T 41246 (see page 25). Millhouses shed always presented a good variety of motive power to delight the enthusiast, but was closed completely five weeks after this photograph was taken.   *David Marriott*

Grimesthorpe Junction was the place where the Midland Railway's new route via Sheffield joined the original Sheffield amd Rotherham railway route from Wicker. In this view looking north can be seen the Firth-Brown steelworks on the left and Engine Shed Sidings on the right. Off the picture to the right is Grimesthorpe MPD, with the Wicker branch diverging on the left just behind the photographer. Jubilee 45662 'KEMPENFELT' is seen hauling a rake of LMS Stanier coaches on a York–Bristol express on 15th May 1952.

Peter Hughes

A TYPICAL SUMMER SATURDAY

Summer Saturdays were always interesting on the Midland line through Sheffield. There was a great variety of motive power and coaching stock to be seen, including types which were not normally seen on Mondays to Fridays. Standard Class 9F 2–10–0s worked on passenger trains as did Class 4F 0–6–0s. A Stanier 2–6–0 from Mold Jn. depot (6B) would usually be found on the Llandudno–Sheffield.

The second Saturday in August was always the busiest day of the year, and the timetabled summer Saturday extras were supplemented by a number of reliefs, some of which were not in the special traffic notice and are denoted by question marks! Late running of trains is not just a present-day problem as the "minutes late" column shows, but no passenger train was more than 50 minutes late. As usual, the poorest timekeepers were the trains from the Western Region.

The date chosen is 9th August 1959. It should be noted that although Scots were to be seen on the Midland by that date, none of them appeared on the day in question, with the heaviest trains being double-headed. As the observations were carried out at Dore & Totley, the locos which worked trains north of Sheffield where there was a loco change at Sheffield are not shown. The times in brackets are the approximate times of unidentified reliefs at Sheffield.

UP TRAINS

Train	From	Arr.	Dep.	To	Mins. Late	Loco(s)
66			10.10	Bangor	T	42931 (1A)
P 456	Carlisle	9.13	10.15	Derby	210	44568 (41B)
249	Hull	10.19	10.25	Birmingham	3	42822 (17B)
74	Bradford	10.32	10.38	London	T	45609 (41C) *Gilbert & Ellice Islands*
78			10.40	Llandudno	T	44716 (2A)
285	Sunderland	10.56	11.01	Bristol	6	73004 (41C)
576†			11.06	Cardiff	7	45413 (8A)
255	Bradford	11.11	11.17	Paignton	8	73011 (41C)
287	Newcastle	11.17	11.24	Cardiff	5	45292 (2E) + 44839 (17A)
975†			12.10	London	2	73170 (55A)
92	Bradford	12.17	12.23	London	T	45557 (14B) *New Brunswick*
2697			12.35	Chinley	T	*
2695			12.36	Nottingham	T	*
2699			12.50	Chinley	T	43863 (41E)
910†	Scarborough	?	(1.05)	?		42826 (17B)
2891	Cudworth	12.58	1.08	Chesterfield	T	42181 (17A)
259	Leeds	1.08	1.24	x. Bristol	6	92008 (21A)
100	Bradford	1.45	1.51	London	T	45615 (14B) *Malay States*
102			2.00	London	T	45626 (17A) *Seychelles*
908†		?	(2.09)	?		44437 (41B)
297	Filey	2.01	2.21	Derby	6	45268 (21A)
2705			2.22	Chinley	T	45280 (21A)
295	York	2.09	2.16	Bristol	28	45685 (82E) *Barfleur*
2709			2.45	Derby	2	61139 (41A)
C 120	Glasgow	3.24	3.30	London	30	44964 (21A)
894†	Newcastle	3.26	3.32	Birmingham	T	92086 (15A)
305	Catterick	3.28	3.34	Birmingham	9	44945 (21A)
C 122	Glasgow	3.36	3.42	London	34	44669 (12A) + 73065 (41C)
307	Newcastle	3.42	3.51	Bristol	18	45519 (82E) *Lady Godiva*
905†	?	?	(4.02)	?		44087 (41B)
2713			4.06	Derby	15	44714 (5A)
2715			4.30	Chinley	T	44174 (41B)
791†	Newcastle		4.38	Birmingham	3	44919 (21A)
C 128	Edinburgh	4.33	4.44	x. Nottingham	18	44985 (14B)
C 130	Edinburgh	4.50	4.56	London	16	73066 (55A)

Train	From	Arr.	Dep.	To	Mins. Late	Loco(s)
309/265	Scarborough	5.02	5.15	Bristol	3	45273 (55A)
2719			5.25	Derby	4	75062 (16A)
2721			5.30	Manchester	2	42452 (9E)
Military	Newcastle		(5.43)	Leicester		45263 (16A)

DOWN TRAINS

Train	From	Arr.	Dep.	To	Mins. Late	Loco(s)
300	Worcester	11.10	11.17	York	5	73139 (17A)
119	Leicester		11.24 D	Blackpool	T	42826 (17B)
214	Bristol	12.05	12.11	Bradford	T	40504 (16A) + 45577 (82E) *Bengal*
938†	Nottingham	12.20	12.26	Edinburgh	1	44985 (14B)
C 852	Blackpool	12.36			7	43940 (21A)
71	London	12.37	12.42	Edinburgh	7	45611 (16A) *Hong Kong*
304	Bristol	12.51	12.57	Newcastle	T	44857 (55A)
75	London	1.10	1.15	Glasgow	3	44757 (55A)
986	London	1.23	1.30	Glasgow	10	44822 (14A)
81	London	1.30	1.37	Glasgow	8	40585 (16A) + 45694 (55A) *Bellerophon*
308	Cardiff	1.40	1.46	Newcastle	34	40489 (85E) + 73068 (82E)
991	Birmingham	1.46	1.52	Newcastle	5	44919 (21A)
1842	Chesterfield	1.59			8	42146 (17A)
2626	Manchester	2.03			T	42813 (21A)
1804	Nottingham	2.25	2.31	Leeds	T	43037 (19C)
870†	Bournemouth?	(2.29)		Leeds		73019 (82F)
216	Weston-Super-Mare	2.32	2.40	x. Newcastle	26	45699 (82E) *Galatea*
218 R/T	Paignton	2.43	2.49	Bradford	T	92104 (15C)
W 661†	Rhyl	2.43			T	45328 (8B)
310 R/T	Bristol	3.11	3.20	Newcastle	39	45572 (82E) *Eire*
95	London	3.24			8	45263 (16A)
W 496	Llandudno§	3.28			T	42767 (9G)
99	London	3.29	3.36	Bradford	28	45683 (41C) *Hogue*
220	Bournemouth	3.39			2	73155 (41C)
W 70	Llandudno	3.44			46	42965 (6B)
314	Paignton	3.56	4.01	Newcastle	46	45576 (41C) *Bombay*
226	Bournemouth	4.08	4.19	Bradford	28	73156 (41B)
2630	Manchester	4.10				42452 (9E) + 46400 (41C)
2632	Nottingham	4.25			T	44200 (18A)
232	Paignton	4.33	4.40	Leeds	32	44962 (21A)
240	Kingswear	4.54	5.01	Bradford	50	45682 (82E) *Trafalgar*
242	Bournemouth	5.03	5.10	Leeds	25	73090 (84G)
5	Blackpool	5.10			T	45276 (8A)
244	Bristol	5.24			27	45608 (55A) *Gibralter*
115	London	5.32			24	45294 (26F)
247	Weston-Super-Mare	5.41			22	44853 (55A)
896†	Exeter	5.41	5.47	Bradford	40	92164 (15C)

NOTES:

† – Relief service
* – Not observed
x. – extended to
§ – Colwyn Bay–Sheffield starting back at Llandudno
R/T – retimed
D – Time at Dore & Totley West Jn.

81/C 122 – THE THAMES–CLYDE EXPRESS
71/C 130 – THE WAVERLEY
240 – THE DEVONIAN
P – Parcels
C – Originated in Central Division of LMR
W – Originated in Western division of LMR

GRIMESTHORPE MPD (19A–later 41B)

▲Around the outside turntable of Grimesthorpe MPD on 23rd May 1952. Left to right are an unidentified Class 5MT 4–6–0, 'Crab' 2–6–0 42904, an LNWR 'Super D' 0–8–0, an unidentified Class 8F 2–8–0, Class 5MT 4–6–0 45262 and Class 4F 0–6–0 44573. Grimesthorpe Junction signal box can be seen in the background.   *Peter Hughes*

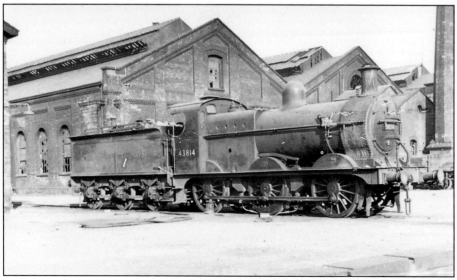

◀The back of the roundhouse on the same day with MR 3F 0–6–0 43814 on the line leading to the fitting shop traverser.
Peter Hughes

Grimesthorpe MPD was opened in 1877 and was officially known as 'Sheffield'. It consisted of a typical MR roundhouse with an eight road fitting shop behind it served by a traverser. There were two coaling stages. In the yard there was a turntable serving a number of roads, in effect an open semi-roundhouse. Its allocation of locos in BR days reflected the fact that its primary duty was to provide locos for freight work, although a number of mixed traffic types, e.g. Stanier Class 5MT 4–6–0s or 'Crab' 2–6–0s were used on seasonal passenger traffic as well as express freight duties. Coded 19A, it became 41B on transfer to the Eastern Region on 1st February 1958. Closure was on 11th September 1961.

ALLOCATION HISTORY OF STEAM LOCOMOTIVES 1st January 1948–11th September 1961.

For notes see page 54.

40324 –06/49.	43335 ?–08/59 (W).	44265 01/55–09/61.	46451 NEW 04/50–04/61.
40401 –06/50.	43341 09/52–09/57 (W).	44275 04/53–06/53.	47228 11/52–06/57.
40411 07/51–10/53.	43361 02/58–03/58, 09/59–10/60 (W).	44284 –04/54.	47235 –08/57.
40728 –07/52 (W).		44285 –04/54.	47236 –07/56.
729 –06/51 (W).	43388 12/53–09/59 (W).	44287 11/52–09/61.	47238 11/51–01/53.
41660 ?–03/52.	43395 02/58–03/58, 09/59–03/61 (W).	44334 –07/54.	47432 –07/57.
41661 07/51–10/51.		44355 –10/50.	47513 –05/61 (W).
41768 –12/49.	43406 02/58–02/60 (W).	44418 –?.	47545 –12/49.
41781 04/48–07/51 (W).	43431 02/58–02/60 (W).	44426 –09/61.	47548 01/48–09/61.
41795 06/56–04/59 (W).	43463 01/49–11/52.	44437 –09/61.	47563 02/50–05/55.
41835 03/60–10/60.	43468 –04/50.	44550 –12/53.	47611 ?–09/56.
41855 –04/48.	43595 –03/57 (W).	44556 –07/54.	47624 –09/61 (W).
41857 –05/59 (W).	43596 –?.	44568 –09/61.	47625 02/60–05/61.
42761 –07/49.	43604 12/48–12/53 (W).	44572 –01/49.	47636 09/54–03/60 (W).
42769 –?, 11/50–01/52.	43605 –01/52.	44573 –03/61.	48007 04/49–06/49.
42794 11/54–07/61.	43607 –06/56 (W).	44664 NEW 07/49–09/49.	48017 –07/49.
42797 –01/51, 08/54–07/61.	43634 05/58–11/60 (W).	44665 NEW 07/49–09/49.	48037 06/59–07/59.
42904 –07/48, 09/48–07/51, 08/51 –12/52, 05/53–04/61.	43636 –05/53.	44802 02/48–05/58.	48105 –01/48.
	43637 10/55–09/61.	44804 07/49–?.	48116 –09/57.
43012 03/54–09/57.	43661 –11/54 (W).	44827 ?–11/50.	48144 05/53–04/55, 12/55–04/61.
43015 05/48–01/52.	43662 –08/53 (W).	44843 07/49–?.	48178 11/57–10/58, 06/59–01/61.
43032 NEW 03/49–09/52.	43669 11/55–09/61.	44845 08/50–10/50.	48179 07/48–05/61.
43037 NEW 06/49–10/50.	43683 –11/54 (W).	44855 05/53–11/56.	48189 12/50–04/61.
43038 NEW 07/49–01/52.	43715 –02/61 (W).	44858 –05/58.	48216 09/52, 05/53–08/53, 03/60–05/61.
43041 NEW 08/49–03/54.	43731 –07/59 (W).	44917 –04/48.	
43042 NEW 09/49–09/57.	43745 09/56–10/58.	44921 –08/50.	48219 –02/52.
43089 02/61–07/61.	43749 –03/60 (W).	44944 07/50–07/57.	48284 –09/52.
43111 11/59–04/61.	43751 12/58–08/61 (W).	44971 –03/48.	48314 –04/53.
43146 01/60–07/61.	43755 –11/55 (W).	45056 10/49–03/54.	48354 –02/48.
43159 11/59–04/61.	43772 –03/50 (W).	45059 10/53–11/54.	48447 02/52–05/54.
43160 02/61–09/61.	43775 –11/55 (W).	45061 –07/50.	48452 02/52–11/55, 01/56–03/57.
43174 02/58–02/60 (W).	43781 09/54–11/55.	45062 11/50–09/57.	48642 –04/61.
43181 11/55–04/57 (W).	43800 05/52–01/61 (W).	45074 ?–11/50.	48765 08/51–05/61.
43203 02/58–09/60 (W).	43844 –03/61 (W).	45088 –01/49.	22950 RN 58139 06/51 –03/53.
43222 03/58–06/59 (W).	44006 –02/48.	45128 ?–12/50.	22951 RN 58140 08/51 –07/57 (W).
43225 05/52–11/52.	44020 01/52–10/53.	45215 –07/50.	22969 (58150) –09/48 (W).
43234 09/59–01/61.	44036 10/58–05/60.	45225 08/50–10/50.	22970 (58151) –04/51 (W).
43241 –05/53.	44037 07/48–?.	45238 12/50–01/54, 07/54–01/55.	2992 RN 58165 05/50 –04/56, 12/58–01/59.
43243 04/55–07/60 (W).	44039 03/56–04/61.	45262 09/48, 10/48–01/55.	
43252 08/53–06/55 (W).	44087 03/57–04/61.	45263 07/49–?.	3031 RN 58190 10/48 –05/57.
43254 11/54–09/61.	44097 02/60–04/61.	45335 11/50–08/54.	3037 RN 58192 06/49 12/50–11/58.
43307 02/58–07/60 (W).	44165 –?.	45407 –03/54.	
43325 11/55–01/56.	44174 09/52–09/61.	45447 07/54–05/56.	3066 (58208) –09/49 (W).
43332 12/53–05/58 (W).	44211 –05/52.	46450 NEW 04/50–03/61.	3101 RN 58220 08/50 –01/56.
43334 –03/56 (W).	44212 –09/61.		

3118	RN 58225 10/48–12/58 (W).	3512	RN 58276 08/49–06/56 (W).	73016	09/51–02/52.		78025	NEW 06/54–11/54.
3140	RN 58232 01/50–05/54 (W).	68497	03/60–09/60 (W).	73043	04/58–04/61.		90418	04/60–04/61.
3171	RN 58244 10/49 04/54–	68569	03/60–03/60.	73074	01/59–04/61.		92189	04/58–05/58.
	05/54 (W).	73000	04/58–01/61.	73156	01/59–09/60.			

MILLHOUSES MPD (19B–later 41C)

◄Compounds were a feature of the Millhouses allocation right until the end (see page 35). LMS Compound 41137 in standard BR line black livery is seen outside the shed in 1953. *Peter Hughes*

NOTES ON DEPOT ALLOCATION LISTS

(W) Withdrawn on date shown.

RN Renumbered on date shown.

NEW Delivered new to depot on date shown.

First and last dates are shown. Where no first date is shown, the loco was at the depot concerned on 1st January 1948.

Where a new BR number is shown in parentheses, this was never carried by the loco concerned.

Where no BR number is shown, the loco was condemned still bearing its LMS number.

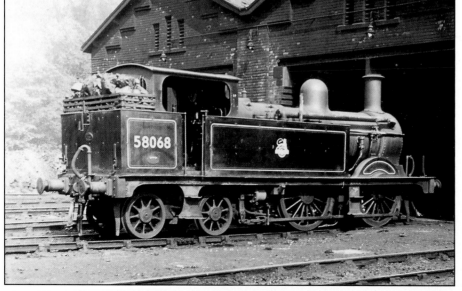

◄Millhouses's fleet of MR Class 1P 0–4–4Ts were withdrawn in 1953. This one, 58068, managed to get a repaint in BR lined black livery, unlike 1370 (see page 7). It is fitted with condensing apparatus, not much use in the Sheffield area. *Peter Hughes*

Millhouses MPD was an eight road straight shed. It was opened in 1901 and its primary purpose was to serve the passenger services, its only freight working being the 81 trip, for which an MR 2F 0–6–0 was allocated. This was later replaced by an Ivatt Class 2MT 2–6–0. In BR days, the fleet of Jubilees was used for the main express workings, backed up by Stanier Class 5MT 4–6–0s. These were later replaced by Standard Class 5MT 4–6–0s which disappeared with the coming of the Royal Scots in 1960. Coded 19B, it became 41C on transfer to the Eastern Region on 1st February 1958. Closure was on 1st January 1962. No diesel locomotives were allocated.

ALLOCATION HISTORY 1st January 1948–1st January 1962

For notes see opposite.

40082 –05/53.	41209 08/53–01/62.	45590 –02/51, 04/51–01/62.	1423 RN 58086 12/48. 02/49–07/49, 08/49–04/50.
40120 04/51–11/53.	41245 NEW 10/49–01/62.	45594 –01/62.	
40139 –08/51.	41246 NEW 10/49–01/62.	45602 09/57–01/62.	3071 RN 58209 07/49. –03/54.
40148 07/56–06/59.	43032 09/52–09/61.	45607 –01/62.	3095 RN 58216 10/49. 03/54–06/56.
40182 10/51–11/51.	43037 05/60–01/62.	45609 09/50–09/60 (W).	
40183 01/50–02/50.	43341 01/49–09/52.	45621 –09/52.	61083 08/61–01/62.
40433 03/57–07/57.	43463 –01/49.	45627 09/60–01/62.	61093 08/61–01/62.
40482 03/57–06/57 (W).	44661 06/53–05/58.	45654 09/50–01/62.	61138 12/59–02/60.
40487 –11/52.	44664 09/49–03/54.	45656 01/51–01/62.	61152 11/59–04/61.
40493 01/49–02/52.	44665 09/49–03/57.	45664 01/48–01/62.	61166 08/61–09/61.
40502 01/49–02/51.	44776 06/53–09/53.	45679 –02/52.	61334 11/59–01/60.
40518 –04/51.	44819 06/56–09/56.	45683 –01/62.	61820 07/61–01/62.
40538 01/51–09/57.	44830 09/53–05/58.	45696 –06/48.	61822 07/61–01/62.
544 –10/49 (W).	44839 06/57–09/57.	45725 09/48–01/62.	61959 07/61–09/61.
545 –12/48 (W).	44847 06/55–05/58.	46131 02/60–01/62.	61989 07/61–09/61.
549 01/50–04/51 (W).	44848 09/53–09/55.	46147 02/60–01/62.	73000 01/53–03/53.
40731 –12/48 (W).	44851 09/53–09/55.	46148 02/60–01/62.	73002 01/60–04/61.
40907 06/53–09/60 (W).	44859 –09/51.	46151 02/60–01/62.	73004 04/58–02/60.
41014 –11/50.	44862 –01/50.	46164 02/60–01/62.	73011 09/53–02/60.
41016 –11/51 (W).	44963 –04/52.	46400 06/56–10/61.	73013 NEW 08/51–09/53.
41021 –12/51.	44964 –03/54.	46450 03/61–01/62.	73014 NEW 09/51–09/53.
41024 –09/48 (W).	44965 –09/52.	46451 04/61–01/62.	73015 NEW 09/51–09/53.
41026 –09/48 (W).	44971 02/48–03/48, 01/49–04/49, 06/49–01/50.	46494 06/56–03/61.	73016 02/52–01/53, 03/53–01/62.
41037 –03/51 (W).		47463 05/55–06/56.	73046 04/58–04/61.
41058 06/53–02/54 (W).	44986 04/50–07/51, 04/52–05/58.	47623 04/55–05/55.	73047 NEW 12/53–07/55.
41062 –09/57.	45056 03/54–05/58.	1249 RN 58033 10/48. –02/48.	73048 NEW 12/53–02/60.
41063 09/50–02/55.	45186 10/54–11/54.	1370 (58067) –02/53 (W).	73065 NEW 10/54–01/62.
41070 11/52–04/56 (W).	45260 10/48–09/51, 06/56–09/56, 06/57–09/57.	1371 RN 58068 11/49. 04/50–10/53 (W).	73067 04/58–02/60.
41071 11/52–11/55 (W).			73073 04/58–02/60.
41072 –10/55 (W).	45264 07/49–09,52, 05/54–09/54.	1377 RN 58071 01/51. –02/53.	73074 07/55–02/56, 03/56–01/59.
41075 04/48–06/50.	45272 07/51–11/51.	1396 RN 58076 04/51. –08/52.	73155 04/58–01/62.
41079 –11/52.	45407 03/54–10/54.	1397 RN 58077 08/49. 10/53–09/54.	73156 04/58–01/59.
41159 12/57–04/58 (W).	45514 12/60–05/61 (W).		78022 NEW 05/54–01/62.
41190 05/52–01/58 (W).	45536 02/60–01/62.	1402 (58078) –05/49 (W).	78023 NEW 05/54–01/62.
41191 05/52–08/55.	45570 06/57–01/62.	1411 RN 58080 08/49. 11/53–04/55.	78024 NEW 05/54–01/62.
41199 07/56–01/58 (W).	45576 08/52–01/62.		78025 11/54–01/62.

Names of Jubilee Class Locomotives:

45570 NEW ZEALAND	45609 GILBERT & ELLICE ISLANDS	45664 NELSON
45576 BOMBAY	45621 NORTHERN RHODESIA	45679 ARMADA
45590 TRAVANCORE	45627 SIERRA LEONE	45683 HOGUE
45594 BHOPAL	45654 HOOD	45696 ARETHUSA
45602 BRITISH HONDURAS	45656 COCHRANE	45725 REPULSE
45607 FIJI		

Note: The names of the Rebuilt Patriots and Royal Scots are shown on page 7.

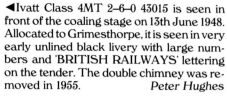

◄Ivatt Class 4MT 2–6–0 43015 is seen in front of the coaling stage on 13th June 1948. Allocated to Grimesthorpe, it is seen in very early unlined black livery with large numbers and 'BRITISH RAILWAYS' lettering on the tender. The double chimney was removed in 1955.   *Peter Hughes*

All sorts of locomotives visited Millhouses from time to time. A particularly interesting working being the thrice-weekly summer Glasgow St. Enoch–London Marylebone car-sleeper. This train changed engines at Beighton in the middle of the night and the incoming loco stabled at Millhouses for the day. Thus a shed visit was essential every Tuesday, Thursday and Sunday. Sundays presented no problem, but on Tuesdays and Thursdays in term time, the author found it was just possible to run from Nether Edge Grammar School to the shed and back in the lunch break. The reward varied. Generally a Corkerhill Jubilee but sometimes a Polmadie Royal Scot or a Britannia.

Clans were observed on a number of occasions. More mundane visitors to Millhouses included LNER designs working in from York, usually B1s, V2s or B16/3s, although generally these stabled at Sheffield Midland.

◄A most unusual visitor was this Selby-allocated unrebuilt NER B16/1 4–6–0 61458 observed during 1956.   *Peter Hughes*

THE BARNSLEY BRANCH

◄For most of the BR steam era, the Barnsley Branch was worked by Ivatt Class 2MT 2–6–2Ts. This service was the only 'push and pull' service to operate into Sheffield Midland, and was operated by Royston locomotives. 41282 is seen awaiting departure with the 10.20 am to Barnsley on 1st August 1957.   *Peter Owen Jones*

▼A major surprise was the allocation of L&YR 2–4–2Ts to the service in 1954. 50646 is seen just before Fife Street, Wincobank on the 4.45 pm Sheffield–Barnsley Court House.   *Peter Hughes*

DORE & TOTLEY WEST JUNCTION

▲Dore & Totley West Junction was the junction where the spur from the main line joined the Hope Valley line. In this view, a Trafford Park Compound 41154 is seen on the 12.50 pm Sheffield–Chinley just passing over the junction in June 1953.

Peter Hughes

◄Taken from the opposite side of the line 'Crab' 2–6–0 approaches the junction with the heavily-loaded 10.30 am Sheffield–Hope ramblers train on a Sunday during July 1953.

Peter Hughes

▲The Dore & Totley South Jn.–West Jn. spur was normally used only for freight but special passenger trains and trains diverted from the Millers Dale route also used it. Stanier Class 5MT 4–6–0 45276 is seen at Dore & Totley West Jn. on a special, probably a Nottingham–Edale Sunday ramblers special. *Peter Hughes*

►Beyer Garratt 2–6–0+0–6–2 47971 from Hasland depot leaves Dore & Totley West Jn. with a coal train from Avenue to Gowhole. *Peter Hughes*

Hasland-based Beyer-Garratt 2–6–0 +0–6–2 47998 approaches Dore Tunnel running light engine back from Gowhole yard to Hasland depot. *Peter Hughes*

Further copies of this publication can be obtained at £4.95 plus 50p postage and packing (£1 overseas) from:

Mail Orders,
Platform 5 Publishing Ltd.,
Lydgate House, Lydgate Lane,
SHEFFIELD, S10 5FH
England.

We hope that you have enjoyed reading this book, the first in our 'Steam Days on BR' series. We would like to hear from anyone who could contribute black & white photographs or colour slides for this series, also from potential authors. All regions of BR will be considered for possible titles. Please write to Peter Fox at the above address. Please do not send actual photographs at this stage.